A Devotional Journey thru the
Patterns of Power
Jesus left for us to Follow

30 Days to
EMPOWERED

by Charlana Kelly

Whole Life
PRESS

30 Days to Empowered
A Devotional Journey thru the
Patterns of Power
Jesus left for us to Follow
© 2023 Charlana Kelly

Scripture quotations are taken from the Holy Bible, New Living Translation, copyright ©1996, 2004, 2015 by Tyndale House Foundation. Used by permission of Tyndale House Publishers, Carol Stream, Illinois 60188. All rights reserved.

Scripture quotations marked TPT are from The Passion Translation®. Copyright © 2017, 2018, 2020 by Passion & Fire Ministries, Inc. Used by permission. All rights reserved. ThePassionTranslation.com.

Publisher:
WholeLife Press a division of SpeakTruth Media Group, LLC PO Box 178, Crockett TX 75835-7448

Book design by SpeakTruth Media Group, LLC.

ISBN: 979-8-9884573-0-5 *(pb)*

Books are available in quantity for promotional or premium use. For information on discounts and terms, please inquire at order@speaktruthmedia.com.

Printed in the USA

For God will never give you

the spirit of fear,

but the Holy Spirit

who gives you mighty power,

love, and self-control.

2 Timothy 1:7, (TPT)

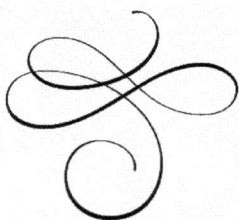

Introduction

If ever there was a time in history when God's people needed to be "led by the Spirit," it is NOW!

We need to hear what God is speaking through the Spirit. We need to obey what the Spirit is leading us to say and do.

It's a Win-Win!

Jesus, being God and man, gave believers a perfect, Spirit-led pattern to follow.

In the pages of this book and over the next 30 days, if you apply what I share, you, too, will walk in the power of the Holy Spirit, just like Jesus did while fulfilling his ministry on earth.

Take time to meditate on the shared verses each day. Think about the message and how you can apply its wisdom in your personal life and relationships.

Consider how you have received what Paul termed in his letter to the Corinthians a "ministry of reconciliation." And how you can partner with God to bring people to Jesus.

If you invest your time to learn how to walk in the power of the Spirit, your life will be empowered, and the power of God working in and through you will be released into the lives of others. Then, you will be a witness to the work of the Spirit in their lives too.

Day One

The Journey

Luke 3:21 - 4:15, In these verses, Jesus was baptized. The Spirit came upon Him. He was FILLED with the Spirit. He was LED by the Spirit into the wilderness and tested for forty days. Then He came out in the POWER of the Spirit.

You are called to the same journey. The Holy Spirit will come upon you and fill you, then lead you in every endeavor, and you will walk IN POWER! Get a revelation of His Holy Spirit power working in you!

Ask Him to lead and guide you. He is your teacher, leader, and guide. The Spirit of Truth! And, He is your friend, your intercessor, and your sweet guarantee of all the promises of God.

Day Two

God Knows You

"*I knew you before I formed you in your mother's womb. Before you were born, I set you apart and appointed you as my prophet to the nations.*" Jeremiah 1:5

God knows you! He has *always* known you, even before you showed up here on Earth!

You were set apart for a purpose when He formed you in your mother's womb. He knows where you are today! You are special to Him because you are His creation —— not an accident, not a second thought, not at all insignificant. The Creator of the Universe KNOWS YOU because He MADE you! And He has a plan and purpose for your life! Let that sink in. Let that encourage you. You are known and seen AND LOVED by God!

Day Three

You Have an Identity in Christ

"*The Spirit is God's guarantee that He will give us the inheritance He promised and that He has purchased us to be His own people. He did this so we would praise and glorify Him.*" Ephesians 1:14

In Christ, you are: Blessed, chosen, holy, blameless, loved, adopted into the Family of God, redeemed, forgiven, filled with Wisdom, unifier of Heaven & Earth, predestined for Glory, and marked with a seal.

Now, get in front of a mirror every day, look yourself square in the eyes, and say out loud, "In Christ, I am blessed, I am chosen, I am holy, I am blameless, I am loved, I am adopted into the family of God, I am redeemed, I am forgiven, I am filled with wisdom, I bring unity, I am predestined for glory, and I am marked by the Holy Spirit.

Day Four

You Are Chosen

"You are a chosen people. You are royal priests, a holy nation, God's very own possession. As a result, you can show others the goodness of God, for he called you out of the darkness into his wonderful light." 1 Peter 2:9

Being chosen sets you apart for something special —— to play on a team, to receive a reward, perhaps to become someone's spouse.

It means you belong!

Now you belong to God, His precious possession. You are in the utmost "In Crowd"! Now you are no longer in the world's darkness but called into God's glorious light. Joy and peace abound in His light and as a result of doing things His way. Take time to consider the benefits of being God's chosen child.

Ask Him to reveal new things to you daily that confirm that within you.

Day Five

Receive the Holy Spirit

"*Did you receive the Holy Spirit when you believed?*" Acts 19:2—6

When Paul visited believers at Ephesus, he learned that not only had they not received the Holy Spirit, they had never even heard of Him either! Perhaps you were like them, but (glory to God!) you know now. Seek Him out. Seeks His gifts. Get familiar with His voice. He will lead you, teach you, and fill you to overflowing with the love of God! Meditate on these truths daily and declare: "Holy Spirit, teach me, lead me, guide me in every part of my life!"

We can only experience what God has given us by first acknowledging the gift, thus becoming aware of the fact that we have received it. Once we become aware, we can behave in such a way as to show God we believe. First, by asking God to help us and asking the Holy Spirit to get involved in whatever the situation is where we need His help.

Go ahead, ask Him right now to get involved in every part of your life and family! He will. Now start listening to hear how He will lead you.

Day Six

Empowered for Daily Life

"For if you live by its dictates, you will die. But if through the power of the Spirit, you put to death the deeds of your sinful nature, you will live." Romans 8:13

    The Israelites had the law (well, lots of laws) and could not keep them. Jesus gave us two commands to fulfill that law, but still, we struggle.

    Even so, there is good news: the Holy Spirit in us empowers us to live a life that pleases God. We make choices every day to live according to our flesh (our sinful nature) or according to the Spirit (our Christ-like nature). By the Holy Spirit's power, we can succeed in obeying God... and live!

    It's by His power that we are transformed into the image and likeness of Christ. Rely on the Holy Spirit to guide you to make daily decisions that lead to life!

Day Seven

Be Bold for Jesus

"*The members of the council were amazed when they saw the boldness of Peter and John, for they could see that they were ordinary men with no special training in the Scriptures. They also recognized them as men who had been with Jesus.*" Acts 4:13

Peter and John garnered much attention because of their bold speech. Those observing them knew that they were uneducated men with no special training. We take comfort in knowing God can use us just as we are. Catch the point here. Focus on what set them apart and emboldened them to speak radically.

They had been with Jesus! Endued with power from the Holy Spirit, they could not help but share the Jesus they had experienced. You, too, have a Jesus experience, and you have been given the Holy Spirit to embolden you to share His Good News!

Allow the Holy Spirit to lead you as you proclaim the goodness of God's love and impact the lives of those around you for Jesus.

Day Eight

The Spirit is Enough, More Than Enough

"Jesus, full of the Holy Spirit, left the Jordan and was led by the Spirit into the wilderness, where for forty days he was tempted[a] by the devil. He ate nothing during those days, and at the end of them, he was hungry." Luke 4: 1-2

Immediately after His baptism, the Spirit led Jesus into the wilderness. For nearly six weeks, satan did everything to get Jesus to fall: tempting and cajoling Him, trying His identity and authority.

During that trial, Jesus submitted Himself to the Spirit. For each temptation, the Spirit prompted Jesus to use the word of God to combat the enemy. Each time it was enough, more than enough.

The verse above tells us that Jesus ate no food throughout His testing. He did not rely on food to satisfy his body. Instead, in the face of a fierce trial, he solely relied on the Spirit of God to sustain Him.

You may not be in a physical wilderness for six weeks with no food. However, you will face trials and temptations that require you to wholly submit yourself to the Spirit of God to make it through. In your most complex challenges, focus on something other than satisfying your flesh. Instead, make God your focus and allow the Holy Spirit to provide your defense. Then, just as Jesus did, you will walk away victorious.

Day Nine

Your Guide to Truth

"When the Spirit of truth comes, he will guide you into all the truth, for he will not speak on his own authority, but whatever he hears, he will speak, and he will declare to you the things that are to come." John 16:13

In John Chapter 14, Jesus told us that the Spirit would remind us of His words. Here, He reveals that the Spirit will give us clarity of what the Scriptures say and that He will guide us into all truth.

The Holy Spirit is our direct link to the mind and heart of Father God. Rejoice! We are no longer on our own to understand God's intent and instructions. The One who created us wants us to be informed. He wants us to be empowered to follow Him.

Loving parents do not leave their children to their own devices, which would bring sure destruction. What a loving Father God we serve!

He will remind you what He said. He will reveal the truth. He will show you things to come. He desires for you to be wise and successful. Why? Because He loves you, His child.

Think about that.

Day Ten

Who's Your Daddy?

"For all who are led by the Spirit of God are sons of God. For you did not receive the spirit of slavery to fall back into fear, but you have received the Spirit of adoption as sons, by whom we cry, "Abba! Father!" The Spirit himself bears witness with our spirit that we are children of God." Romans 8:14-15

Love. Family. Children. These concepts are important to God. So important that He sent His son into a family. Jesus could have appeared as an adult, ready to do ministry, but no, He was born just like every person who has lived.

Some of us know a family from experience, yet for some, that experience is not love at all. Because of God's great love for us, His children, the Holy Spirit reveals that we have been adopted, chosen, loved, and set apart. He wants us to know without a doubt that He has taken us in, enjoined us to His family and that we are His children.

We can freely call on Him, rely on Him, and forever know we are loved. We are His. The Holy Spirit will never let us forget that.

Meditate on your relationship with Father God. Do you call Him 'Abba"? Abba means Daddy. He wants to be your Daddy and desires that you know how much you are loved. Think about that today.

Day Eleven

People Will Talk

"*Then Jesus, full of the Holy Spirit, returned from the Jordan River. He was led by the Spirit in the wilderness.*" Then "*Jesus returned to Galilee, filled with the Holy Spirit's power. Reports about him spread quickly through the whole region.*" Luke 4:1 & 14

When you are filled with the Holy Spirit, expect results! The raw wilderness, satanic temptation, and even physical hunger had no victory over Jesus. In that trial, He was fully man and faced those things as a man. His victory was not because He was God but because He was full of the Holy Spirit.

In Galilee later, people were talking about Him. And they were not talking about how He looked but about what He did! He was filled with power and went about teaching, preaching, and healing! The infilling and empowerment of the Holy Spirit in you will produce action and bring results.

Yield yourself to Him. Invite Him to act in your life and your circum-stances. Expect Him to bring HIS results. You will see the miraculous overtake the mundane! Oh, and do not be surprised when people talk...it won't be about how you look!

Day Twelve

Oh, say, Can You See?

"The Spirit of the Lord is upon me, for he has anointed me to bring Good News to the poor. He has sent me to proclaim that captives will be released, that the blind will see, that the oppressed will be set free and that the time of the Lord's favor has come."
Luke 4: 18 & 19

These verses should excite you! Have you heard the good news? Were you set free? Have your eyes been opened? Is your oppression broken off? Are you immersed in the Lord's favor? Shout "Yes and Amen!"

Jesus saw Himself in this prophecy from Isaiah and, full of the Spirit and power, began to walk in the fullness of His ministry. But there is more! Jesus then gave that same Spirit and power to each of us who believed! See Luke 9:1. Not only have we received, but now we are empowered to GIVE.

Reread this passage. Let these words pour over you. Ask the Holy Spirit for revelation to see yourself in these words. You are anointed to bring good news, deliver freedom, impart vision, and break off chains of oppression. Hallelujah!

Day Thirteen

Are You Smarter Than a Fifth Grader?

"*Then he opened their minds to understand the Scriptures.*" Luke 24:45

Jesus taught the Scriptures throughout his ministry. We read where they opened the scroll of the Torah and taught from it. He opened the Word to the disciples. Now, before His ascension into heaven, that practice shifted.

This verse shows that Jesus opened the disciples to the Word. Because of the Spirit in them, believers could comprehend the scriptures from the inside out. He opened our understanding. That allows us to understand in a way we could not when we only heard the Word from others. Now we can comprehend it for ourselves! We can read the written word and discern it as the living voice of God directly to us! He reiterates this to us in 1 John 2:20, "*But you have an anointing from the Holy One, and you know all things.*"

Let that sink in. By His Spirit, you can know all the things God has for you! Glory to God!

Day Fourteen

You Could not Hear a Pin Drop

"...And many who had been paralyzed or lame were healed. 8 So there was great joy in that city." Acts 8:7b – 8

There is an old joke where someone asks the man why he is banging his head on the wall. He answers because it feels so good when I stop. To appreciate feeling good, one must compare it to feeling bad.

Now imagine these people who were lame or paralyzed, immobile or immovable, stuck and dependent. Most of us never experience the depths of their suffering. When the power of the Holy Spirit fell on them, and each received their healing, you could not hear a pin drop!

No, they were exuberant and noisy. They were leaping and praising God. And not only them but all who had cared for and loved them rejoiced.

The joyful energy born from their restoration was contagious! Others saw it. Others felt it. Others desired it. Think about the miraculous. Think about the spectacular. Become familiar with old things being made gloriously new.

Position yourself to receive a miracle for yourself AND others. Then, get ready to make some joyful noise unto the Lord when the miracle happens!

Day Fifteen

First... Love

"*Jesus saw the huge crowd as he stepped from the boat, and he had compassion on them and healed their sick.*" Matthew 14:14

Jesus was moved with compassion for the people He saw: tender mercies, feelings of affection, deep sympathy, and even pity. His genuine care for the throngs around Him motivated His action to heal them.

First Corinthians 16:14 (TPT) instructs us, "*Let love and kindness be the motivation behind all that you do.*" God does not expect us to love out of our ability because "*The love of God has been poured out in our hearts by the Holy Spirit who was given to us*" (Romans 5:5).

Do you want to walk in the miraculous? First... love.

Are you pursuing the spectacular through the Spirit? First... love.

Desperate to bring deliverance from demons? First... love.

Day Sixteen

Say what?

"I tell you the truth, anyone who believes in me will do the same works I have done, and even greater works because I am going to be with the Father." John 14:12

Wow. This verse is hard to believe; do the same works as Jesus and even greater works? It is impossible to believe if you think about doing those things with your strength! But Jesus did not end His sentence there. Praise the Lord!

Because He went to the Father, the Holy Spirit could come to us, fill and empower us. We have been gifted to continue His ministry here on earth – preaching, teaching, and healing.

You can relax. It is not about you. It is about the Spirit filling you and empowering you to complete His purpose in this world.

Do the same work? Even greater works? Yep. And you can get excited about that!

Believe, do, and witness the miracles as you GO!

Day Seventeen

You have been Called!

"Therefore I, a prisoner for serving the Lord, beg you to lead a life worthy of your calling, for you have been called by God. Always be humble and gentle. Be patient with each other, making allowance for each other's faults because of your love." Ephesians 4:1 & 2

You no longer have to struggle to know if you are called by God. You are!

Callings lead to various places and deliver unique outcomes. "Variety is the spice of life," so be willing to be different! But just as all cakes have a foundation of similar ingredients (flour, sugar, shortening), foundational traits will be evident when we walk worthy of our calling. Humility and gentleness and patience and grace to cover faults. The unconditional love of others.

These actions will result from the work of the Holy Spirit in you. These attitudes and behaviors allow you to lead a life worthy of God's calling.

Pray that you may walk worthy of the calling of the Lord, and He will see to it that you are fruitful in every good work.

Day Eighteen

You have been Equipped!

"*By his divine power, God has given us everything we need for living a godly life. We have received all of this by coming to know him, the one who called us to himself by means of his marvelous glory and excellence.*" 2 Peter 1:3

If you took a position as a firefighter, you would be willing to go to work if they provided you with the right equipment to do your job. You would expect to be trained and given what you need to be successful in your new endeavor. In the same way, when we come into the kingdom of God and choose to serve Him, we can expect He will help us fulfill our role with Him. God has divinely equipped you and supplied all you need to live a godly life. He plans that you get to know Him more intimately so that you can do well the job He gave you. He wants you to come close to Him and partake of His glory and excellence. He wants your success, both for your benefit and for the benefit of others. You can rest in the fact that God is more than a good "boss," He is a good Father and makes sure that you have no lack to complete what He has for you to do.

Day Nineteen

You have been Commissioned!

"Go into all the world and preach the Good News to everyone." Mark 16:15

Go? Okay, I can do that one. Into all the world? Umm... maybe. Preach? Hmmm, hold on. To everyone? No way!

Mark 16;15 is probably one of the Bible's most "rebutted" verses. People read it and say, "But... but...but...!" Let's look at it from a different perspective.

God wants us to think as He thinks. The Bible is full of superlatives; all have sinned and fallen short of the glory of God; the Lord desires that none die without secured salvation; that whosoever believes.

Jesus thinks in global terms, with no limits. The Word says we have the mind of Christ; therefore, we need to think like Jesus on this one. Every believer has been given the directive to tell everyone.

Rather than focusing on what you cannot do, ask God to give you a vision of what you can do. Where can you go? To whom can you share? Who is your part of everyone? God will reveal your role, and the Holy Spirit will empower you to do it! All for the glory of God! Say, "Amen!"

Day Twenty

Prayer is Key, So Ask

"*And whatever you ask in My name, that I will do, that the Father may be glorified in the Son. If you ask anything in My name, I will do it.*" John 14:13 & 14

A Power of Attorney is "The authority to act for another in specified or all matters." Holding power of attorney allows one to act using another person's name as if you were that person!

It is astonishing that Jesus has given us power of attorney and that we can, by right and authority, use His name to accomplish what He wills. That is big! However, if you have that authority and do not use it, it is as though you do not have it at all. But look closer at this verse. It does not instruct us to think in His name; He will do it. No, we must *ask* to get results. That sounds so sensible, yet here Jesus told us not once but twice to ask.

Again, in James 4, we read that we do not have because we do not ask, and in Philippians 4, we are instructed to let our requests be made known to God!

Become accustomed to asking in Jesus' Name. Utilize His sovereign authority to accomplish what He would accomplish. Only when we ask will He do so the Father will be glorified.

Praise the Lord!

Day Twenty-One

Signs will Follow Those who Believe!

"I tell you the truth, anyone who believes in me will do the same works [signs] I have done, and even greater works [signs], because I am going to be with the Father."
John 14:12

The same works that Jesus did? Even greater works? Oh my! Jesus must have known that our mouths would drop open with that, so He prefaced it with, "Hey, I'm telling you the truth!"

There should be no surprise here. He gave us the Holy Spirit to indwell us, teach, and empower us. He gave us the authority to use His Name. He gave us instructions to ask, go, and do. We have everything we need to impact the world and, more important, so that He can change the hearts and lives of the people around us.

We should expect miracles. Why? Because He said so! Close your gaping mouth and stand up, *Empowered Woman*! We've got Kingdom business to do!

Day Twenty-Two

In Jesus' Name, You Will Heal The Sick

"These miraculous signs will accompany those who believe... They will be able to place their hands on the sick, and they will be healed." Mark 15:17a & 18b

Jesus has positioned us for miracles! He has given us the Spirit and the authority of His Name. He called us, told us to ask, and promised us the results. Everything we need is already ours to use and to give to others. The question now is simple: Are you willing to obey? Will you ask? Will you lay hands on the sick? When you do, miracles, signs, and wonders will happen!

The miraculous has nothing to do with you but everything to do with Jesus. Get a revelation of what you are called to do. Stand up in holy boldness to do what

He told you to do. People are suffering and dying for want of a touch from Jesus!

You have the mandate to bring what they need in Jesus' Name! Do not let anything hold you back, not disobedience, not fear, and indeed no doubt! Be bold!

Walk in the POWER of the Spirit! Jesus would not have it any other way.

Day Twenty-Three

Bring Deliverance to Those Who Are Bound

"*One day, as we were going down to the place of prayer, we met a slave girl who had a spirit that enabled her to tell the future... This went on day after day until Paul got so exasperated that he turned and said to the demon within her, "I command you in the name of Jesus Christ to come out of her." And instantly, it left her.*" Acts 16:16 & 18

She was immediately healed when the Holy Spirit directed Paul to end this girl's nonsense. The harassing demon had to yield to the name of Jesus. Paul was exasperated; another translation says he was greatly annoyed. Paul grew tired of seeing this girl suffer, and he rose with an attitude in the name of Jesus! He turned to the devil and took control.

Many people are bound today by emotional and psychological issues and addiction. They are destructive and desperate. Drugs flow freely, both legal and illegal because people medicate what they do not understand, often masking the spiritual roots of their problems.

Jesus came to set the captives free. It is time for us to get feisty with the enemy! Like Paul, get an attitude that says, "No more bondage, satan!" Be willing to confront demonic forces that hold our brothers and sisters captive. Be ready to declare: "I command you in the name of Jesus to 'come out'!" Jesus will handle the rest.

Day Twenty-Four

The Dead Will Live Again!

"*Seated in a window was a young man named Eutychus, who was sinking into a deep sleep as Paul talked on and on. When he was sound asleep, he fell to the ground from the third story and was picked up dead. Paul went down, threw himself on the young man, and put his arms around him. "Don't be alarmed," he said. "He's alive!" ... The people took the young man home alive and were greatly comforted.*" (Acts 20:9, 10, & 12)

Get comfortable with verses that say heal the sick and (gulp!) raise the dead! When we truly understand that Jesus overcame death and the grave, and He bequeathed that power to us through His Spirit, we can build our faith to be obedient when the time comes. Nothing can hold back that power in us; in Jesus' name, we will raise the dead.

Will you be ready to declare, "Come alive in the Name of Jesus!"?

Day Twenty-Five

And Suddenly, They Will See, Hear, Be Saved, And Live!

"I have declared the former things from the beginning; They went forth from My mouth, and I caused them to hear it. Suddenly I did them, and they came to pass." Isaiah 48:3

God is moving in this end time; we see signs & miracles everywhere. He will work on the hearts of man to hear and see in a way they never have before. He will move by His Spirit so that multitudes will be saved, and they will live!

Ask God to reveal your role in this last move of the Holy Spirit. Study to show yourself approved and always be ready to answer anyone who asks you to give a reason for the hope of Jesus in you.

The time is short before Jesus calls us out of this world. The time is now! Get excited to be a laborer in His great harvest that is upon us.

People may not realize it now, but their lives depend on it!

Day Twenty-Six

Open Your Mouth & Speak

"Speak up for those who cannot speak for themselves; ensure justice for those being crushed. Yes, speak up for the poor and helpless, and see that they get justice."
Proverbs 31:8 & 9

Today we live in a culture with an astounding number of voices being heard on television, movies, and get this, 128 social media platforms used by 4 billion people. The noise and chaos of thought they create can make it easy for us to forget that there are still people who have no voice.

Children come to mind first; the unborn, those in poverty, being trafficked, isolated, and alone. Then there are people oppressed by mental illness or addictions, the homeless or displaced, widows, and orphans. The list is long.

As believers, we must look out for "the least of these" and bring attention to their needs. The book of James tells us that when we make a difference in their time of trouble for widows and orphans, we are fulfilling faithful ministry. Do not be silent when you know the Spirit is prompting you to speak.

Ask God to reveal the right words, then boldly step forward. Do not complain and point the finger; go to the one who has the power to bring change. You don't just have the ear of the Creator and King; you will also gain the ear of earthly authorities.

Day Twenty-Seven

Lifetime Guarantee

"God identified us as his own by placing the Holy Spirit in our hearts as the first installment that guarantees everything, He promised. 2Corinthians 1:21 & 22

Great satisfaction comes when you purchase an item with a guarantee. It means that no matter what, the one who made the product promises to fulfill everything they said the product would.

God has given us a guarantee of His promises, and we can rest assured that what He provided will be fulfilled, either now or in the coming time! He has given us His Holy Spirit to remind us of what He said and to be our Comforter who seals and reassures us of the future.

No need to worry, doubt, or fear because the Creator will make good on what He has promised. We have a surety from Him through the presence of His Spirit in us.

Think about that. The words "Lifetime Guarantee" will take on a whole new meaning! We can rejoice that those words apply to our future in heaven with Him!

Day Twenty-Eight

You are Who He says You Are

"*For in Him, we live and move and exist. As some of your own poets have said, 'We are his offspring.'*" Acts 17:28

Have you heard the new song, "*I am who I am because the I Am tells me who I am*"?

There is so much truth in those words. God the Father, through His son Jesus, gives us our identity. We are adopted sons and daughters of the Highest. We have a future and hope because of His love for us (Jeremiah 29:11).

Our lives have worth because of what Jesus was willing to pay to purchase us. Our eternity is fixed and secure because Jesus conquered death and gave us eternal life.

He says I am saved. He says I am forgiven. He says I am free. He says I am healed. He says I am forever His!

Now, those are reasons to REJOICE! Hallelujah!

Day Twenty-Nine

Be Confident in Him

"I pray that God, the source of hope, will fill you completely with joy and peace because you trust in him. Then you will overflow with confident hope through the power of the Holy Spirit." Romans 15:13

Get that! God is the source of hope! When you trust Him, your hope will be like a well springing up and gushing forth with the hope that is *more than enough*. And He gave you His peace, too, unlike the world's peace, which is fleeting at best. That's BIG friend.

The Word also says that we have *joy* unspeakable and full of glory, and in His presence is fullness of joy. And flowing from this joy, peace, and hope is our complete confidence that God is whom He says He is, that Jesus did what He said He did, and that the Holy Spirit fills and holds and leads us day by day. I call that blessed assurance!

Let's sing the old hymn together: *Blessed assurance, Jesus is mine. Oh, what a foretaste of glory divine! Heir of salvation, purchase of God, Born of His Spirit, washed in His blood. This is my story. This is my song. Praising my Savior all the day long!*

God's peace leaves you praising Him forever with the joy of the Lord!

Day Thirty

Go, Tell

"Do not be afraid," said Jesus. *"Go and tell..."*
Matthew 28:10

Peter and John received the Holy Spirit at Pentecost and radically preached Jesus, causing quite a stir. When officials called them in and forbade them to speak about Jesus, they responded, *"We cannot help speaking about what we have seen and heard"* (Acts 4:20).

They.
Could not.
Stop.
Speaking.

Jesus left us simple instructions before He left. Go and tell. He did not ask us to memorize lots of scripture, buy a suit and tie, or take public speaking lessons. Nope.

Just go and tell. We each have an experience with Jesus, each of our stories is different, and each of our stories is important. Somebody needs to hear about your Jesus. Somebody needs to overcome what you overcame.

Go and tell. Jesus prefaced that with "Do not be afraid," so do not be. Go and tell. The Holy Spirit will be with you and lead you to the ones you need to share with.

Be bold. God is with you.

Go, tell.

Closing

If you have made it this far, I know your life has been profoundly changed.

You see, reading, internalizing, memorizing, believing, and putting to practice God's Word opens a door for the Holy Spirit to teach, train, lead, and guide you. Romans 10:17 says, "FAITH comes by hearing and HEARING by the Word of God."

We hear repeatedly by reading and listening to the Scriptures or promises. It builds our faith in God. It increases our confidence and gives us the determination to finish our life strong in Him. And, because of our continued growth, the enemy does not have a chance to deceive and destroy us.

Not only do we grow, but the way we live our lives spurs others on to do the same. Your life will preach the Gospel daily, and when others have challenges, they know whom to ask for prayer and counsel.

In closing, I say to you, "Go! Do the work of an evangelist. Fulfill what God has created you to do."

Now, live empowered by the Spirit every day of your life.

About the Author

Charlana inspires leaders worldwide, teaching them how to engage the current culture to restore the lost art of assertive, influential communication that opens the door for others to hear and consider more profound wisdom in hopes of changing their minds.

In the era of cancel culture, it is vital...no! It's imperative that Christians learn how to bring the right answers into every encounter.

Passionate about mentoring Christian leaders, forging strong relationships, birthing strategic leadership plans, and impacting cultural arenas with Christ, Charlana has worked with church, government, business, finance, and nonprofit leaders to bring clarity and authenticity to their mission.

Charlana is the Founder & CEO of SpeakTruth Media Group. Her radio program, *Unshakable with Charlana Kelly*, is heard daily coast-to-coast on Wilkins Radio Network, Starnes Media Group, and KIVY.

A multiple-time author, Charlana has traveled the world speaking to leaders in multiple nations about engagement and influence.

Charlana also works with aspiring Christian authors, many of whom affectionately call her "The Book Doula."

Want more information? Visit, charlanakelly.com/thebookdoula

She and her husband, Charles, live on the historic King's Highway in the Piney Woods of east Texas.

Charlana loves to hear from you about how her messages have impacted your life in Christ.

Let's connect!

Via **TEXT**: 936-931-7770

On **social media**: @charlanakelly

Listen weekly to
Unshakable w Charlana Kelly
on all Podcast Platforms

Watch **Engage for Influence** on-demand at:
youtube.com/c/charlanakellytv

Via **website**:
unshakablewithcharlanakelly.com

Book Charlana **to Speak** via inquiries to:
bookcharlana@speaktruthmedia.com